DON'T QUIT

Motivation to Reach Your Goals

Dr. Mary J. Huntley

ALL RIGHTS RESERVED
© 2019 by Dr. Mary J. Huntley
Published by Vision to Fruition Publishing House
www.vision-fruition.com

ISBN: 978-0-578-51099-6

Cover Design By: Dr. Mary J. Huntley
Photo Credit: Jackie Hicks
Makeup Artist: Letitia Thornhill

All rights reserved. No part of this book may be reproduced in any form, stored in a retrieval system or transmitted in any form by any means – electronic, mechanical, photocopy, recording or otherwise – without prior written permission of the author.

You may order copies of this book and other materials at **www.drmaryjhuntley.com**

The following translations have been used:

Scriptures taken from the *HOLY BIBLE KING JAMES VERSION* are taken from the Full Study Bible © 1992 Life Publishers International.

Scriptures taken from the *HOLY BIBLE: NEW INTERNATIONAL VERSION.* Copyright © 1973, 1978, 1984 International Bible Society. Used by permission of Zondervan Publishing House. All rights reserved.

Scriptures taken from *THE AMPLIFIED® BIBLE*. Old Testament Copyright © 1965, 1987, by the Zondervan Corporation. The Amplified New Testament Copyright © 1958, 1987 by the Lockman Foundation. Used by permission. (www.Lockman.org)

LET'S CONNECT:

www.drmaryjhuntley.com
Facebook: DrMary J Huntley
Twitter: drmaryj_huntley
Instagram: authordrmaryjhuntley

CONTRIBUTING AUTHOR IN:

**#1 Amazon Bestseller Faith for Fiery Trials: Testimonies That Will Ignite the Fire in Your Soul and Increase Your Faith in God
by Elder Nicole S. Mason, Esquire**

Entrepreneurial Elevation by Cheryl Wood (July 2019)

#1 International Bestseller Voices of the 21st Century: Women Who Influence, Inspire and Make A Difference by Gail Watson

The Purposed Woman 365 Devotional by Latasha Williams

Dedication

This book is dedicated to:

My husband of 45 years, **Dr. Ronald Lee Huntley** who's the love of my life next to my Lord and Savior Jesus Christ, and he is the man I dated exclusively for 6 years before marriage. I am honored to be your wife and I love you very much. THANK YOU for your unending support, and your endless, unconditional love.

My mom, **Mrs. Carrie Lee Edwards**, THANK YOU for leaving me a rich legacy of faith in God and prayer. Thank you for regularly taking me to church at a very early age to ensure that I was spiritually grounded. Thank you for every sacrifice you made for me as a single mom. I am eternally grateful.

The loving memory of my grandmother, **Mrs. Carrie James**, THANK YOU for accepting and receiving me when I was discharged from the hospital after birth. Thank you for allowing me to rest in your arms surrounded by your genuine love. THANK YOU for welcoming me into your home once again when my mom and I moved to Washington, DC. You took precious time to nurture me during the years. Thank you for relinquishing a job to me to ensure that I would earn money to support myself. THANK YOU for a rich legacy of faith in God, love, awesome work ethics, and integrity. I am so grateful for every sacrifice you made so that I could realize my dreams. It was an honor to be in your room while you transitioned to be with the Lord.

My siblings, **Barbara, Calvin and Ronnie,** I love you to the moon and back, and then some more. Thanks for sharing my journey.

The loving memory of **Mrs. Bertha Lee Huntley,** A.K.A. THE BEST mother-in-love in the world. THANK YOU for your unconditional love. You always treated me as your biological daughter. You always made me feel loved and appreciated. You were always in my "front row" to cheer for me and to celebrate my accomplishments.

Faith For Fiery Trials: **Visionary Elder Nicole S. Mason, Esquire, Co-Authors Debbie Andrews, Rhonda Bunch-Turner, Min. Taneshia Curry, Coach Renee Dantzler, Min. Mary Harris, Kisha Martin-Burney, Elder Cheryl Mercer, Elder Angela Minor, Esquire, Tracey Simms Washington (deceased), Charlotte Avery, Crystal Y. Davis, Pastor Joyce Gilmer, Min. Sharon Jamison, Dr. Vikki Johnson, Min. Beverly Lucas, Bershan Shaw, and Cheryl Wood.**

Kristal Clark, CEO of Rock Paper Scissors Foundation and Board President **Carla Yarborough** for your unconditional love and support.

Apostle James Mills and Pastor Vanessa Mills, THANK YOU for your unconditional love and support for over 20 years. THANK YOU for providing an awesome opportunity to serve under your dynamic leadership.

My **#ImpactNation tribe, friends, colleagues, and associates**, THANK YOU for your support.

SPECIAL THANK YOU to **Dr. Tasheka Green** for your continued support and for purchasing the first copy of *Don't Quit*. Continue to "go where God leads and walk in your purpose."

> **A WINNER NEVER QUITS, AND A QUITTER NEVER WINS!**

D
O
N'
T

To:
_____

From:
_____

Date:
_____

Q
U
I
T!

Table of Contents

Foreword 2

Introduction 6

Chapter 1 BELIEVE YOU CAN 8

Chapter 2 SET S.M.A.R.T. GOALS 28

Chapter 3 DO WHAT YOU LOVE 56

Chapter 4 STAY IN YOUR LANE 72

Chapter 5 KEEP IT MOVING 88

Conclusion 98

Appendix A MOTIVATIONAL QUIZ 100

Appendix B S.M.A.R.T. GOAL WORKSHEET 106

Appendix C ENCOURAGING SCRIPTURES 110

About the Author 112

About the Publisher 114

Foreword

It is with great pleasure that I write this Foreword for a woman that I greatly admire! Before I can proceed to talk about this amazing book that Dr. Mary has written with you in mind, it is important for me to speak about the person.

The moment I met Dr. Mary I knew there was something very special about her. For starters, we were attending an awards ceremony, and she was there to support one of the honorees. I knew in that moment that she was truly the kind of woman that I wanted to be in my community of women, who are movers and shakers in their respective industries and vocations and thrive off supporting each other.

Secondly, in the few moments that Dr. Mary and I had to chat, she was warm and encouraging. I have come to know that Dr. Mary is a powerful woman of God, domestic violence awareness advocate, and Certified Master Life Coach. She has been recognized on numerous occasions for the work she does with women to change their lives by helping them to change their perspectives, turn their pain into purpose, and learn to thrive after being knocked down by life's circumstances.

Dr. Mary has proven to be a consistent force of motivation and encouragement in my life. I can always count on her for prayer, positive text messages, and emails, and motivating messages on social media, all designed to motivate and encourage me and every other recipient of her positive energy!

So, it is not a surprise to me that Dr. Mary's inaugural solo project, **DON'T QUIT: *Motivation to Reach Your Goals***, is filled with motivation to move you forward and lay out a strategy to help you bring the vision to pass that God has given you. It is YOUR TIME NOW! Your season is upon you, and Dr. Mary is the Certified Master Life Coach to help you manifest your goals in the Earth today!

The journey that you are embarking upon as you turn the pages in this book will be riveting, refreshing and rewarding. I also have to tell you that you will have to put action with your faith, because Dr. Mary will push you and provide you with a way to connect with her as a resource to help you unravel what has heretofore been tangled and unrecognizable. She will push you from being "stuck" to "soaring." Here is a glimpse of the kind of motivation contained in the pages to follow:

"RECIPE FOR SUCCESS: *Heat up an idea; Take action; Mix it with passion and belief; Then add a dash of persistence."*

You must actively engage in the work that Dr. Mary has included in the pages to come. She writes, *"In order to fulfill your preordained purpose, stay in your lane, and do what you love. This will be far less stressful than trying to fit in someplace that does not fulfill your purpose. You will have passion as your fuel to finish the journey."* I am confident that this book will not only bless you but will also cause you to be a blessing to those you are called to serve. You have taken the first step in your divine destiny by purchasing this book.

Set your mind, heart, and spirit to receive divine instruction, and be intentional about actively engaging in the process. Your Certified

Master Life Coach, Dr. Mary J. Huntley, has poured divine downloads onto the following pages that I am confident will add value to your life, impart wisdom into your heart and ignite purpose in your soul.

Elder Nicole S. Mason, Esquire
Coach and Confidante to High Achieving Women
www.nicolesmason.com

Introduction

"Don't put off until tomorrow what you can do today."
~Abraham Lincoln

"You may delay, but time will not."
~Benjamin Franklin

"Success is not obtained overnight. It comes in installments; you get a little bit today, a little bit tomorrow until the whole package is given out. The day you procrastinate, you lose that day's success."
~Isrealmore Ayivor

All these quotes convey a very similar message. Don't put things off for later. In other words, do not procrastinate. Are you an individual who always puts off things for later? Have there been times when you felt you lacked the motivation, confidence and the skills required to reach your goal? Well, I have great news for you. **You are not alone**. I think that it is safe to say that almost everyone encounters this challenge at some point in life. But, please remember that you don't have to stay stuck.

Don't Quit was written to help you rise to the occasion, as well as to educate, equip, empower, and encourage you to reach your fullest potential. You will be motivated in areas where you initially fell short, and your self-confidence will help you avoid procrastination. You will also be empowered to embark upon new ventures that will leave you fulfilled as you meet a very important intrinsic need of self-esteem.

Social psychologist, Abraham Maslow, Ph.D., created the Hierarchy of Human Needs, which includes various levels indicating man's daily needs. Self-actualization is listed at the top of the Hierarchy of Human Needs and is defined as a person's motivation to reach his or her full potential. Very important to note however is that the basic needs of food, water, and shelter must be met before self-actualization is reached or realized. Once the basic needs are met, then we can start our journey of reaching upward on the hierarchy to ensure the other needs are met.

Therefore, self-confidence and motivation will enable you to succeed and reach your fullest potential. Your self-confidence will be so contagious until it will spill over and attract others. Your friends and colleagues should note a considerable difference in your behavior and attitude after you execute your new plan of action. Most importantly, you will walk with more confidence. Since we are talking about motivation, know that it is the vehicle on which passion travels. Passion also provides that necessary inner drive to help you achieve your goals. So, look no further! Step into the arena of empowerment and confidence building as you see your dreams become a reality.

Chapter One
Believe You Can

In order to get motivated to achieve your goals, you must first believe that you can.

In order to get motivated to achieve our goal, you must first believe that you can. As a preliminary before you start your journey, take the **MOTIVATION QUIZ (Appendix A)** in the back of the book. This will be utilized as a measuring tool for you to chart your progress. You will also take the quiz after you have reached your first goal so that you celebrate your achievement. Keep in mind that success is a journey not a destination.

> *Success is a journey not a destination.*

You were equipped with all the necessary tools to reach your preordained purpose before you left God's assembly line. This fact is corroborated in God's Word. Even though you may not have the support of friends, family or coworkers; **believe in yourself**. Since our great God is for you, it really doesn't matter who tries to come against what you were called to do for the Kingdom of God. Therefore, if you must get up every morning and say to yourself "I can do it," then encourage yourself. You are worth it! Tell yourself, "I can, I must, and I shall do this. I refuse to give up." It doesn't matter how many noisome pestilences or naysayers try to dissuade you from your positive self-talk. Tell the negative committee in your mind to sit down and shut-up because according to Philippians 4:13:

> ***I can do all things*** *[which He has called me to **do**]* ***through*** *Him who strengthens and empowers me [to fulfill His purpose-I **am** self-sufficient **in Christ's** sufficiency; I **am** ready for anything and equal to anything **through** Him who infuses me with inner strength and confident peace.]* AMP

Let's take a closer look at this scripture. It states that I can do all things. Since all leaves out nothing and no thing, with faith in God you can do it. Next, notice that it emphasizes the things that God has called you to do. God has given each of us specific assignments in order that we bring Him all the glory. Therefore, rest assured that our Omniscient Father would never set you up to fail. He knew what you needed and has so graciously provided for you. Receive the faith of Abraham, knowing that when God could swear by no other, He "swore by Himself." And since He called you, know that He has strengthened, equipped, and empowered you to fulfill your purpose. So, child of the Most High God, know that you are more than a conqueror through Christ Jesus. Know that you are ready for anything that comes your way because God infused you with inner strength and confident peace. Rest assured that God is your source and total resource. You don't have to exclusively depend on your ability to get the job done. That is enough to infuse you with enough positivity and ignite the fire within your soul to help you reach your goal.

God has already done the heavy lifting. He knows our frailties, our strengths, and weaknesses. In Jeremiah 1:5 God says:

Before I formed you in the womb, I knew you [and approved of you as My chosen instrument]. AMP

Since He knows you, just cooperate with His perfect plan for your life. Depend on Him to get you through the process of becoming more motivated to reach your goals. Encourage yourself with the following recipe:

> **RECIPE FOR SUCCESS:**
> Heat up an **idea**. Take **action**.
> Mix it with **passion** and **belief**;
> Then add a dash of **persistence**.

Daily remind yourself that you are flawlessly executing your action plan. And, on those days when you may feel as if you cannot take another step, just know that we have all had to pick ourselves up and carry on—eventually reaching our goal. Continue to reflect upon Philippians 4:13 to get back on course.

Positivity is key to reaching any goal. Just as you reflected upon Philippians 4:13 and analyzed its importance to reach your goal, you can also do the same with other encouraging scriptures. **(See Appendix C)** Whether you make notecards or read and record positive scriptures for your daily use, just know that they will play a very important role in helping you reach your goal. This process can also possibly help you memorize scriptures that you have attempted to memorize in the past. Christians have the power to create a positive environment by speaking life as stated in Proverbs 18:21. Your tongue is a creative force that can be utilized to help you reach your goal. **Never** underestimate the power, and authority you must change a negative situation or environment into a positive one. Therefore, this method could prove to be a bonus. A very rewarding method could be to incorporate the scripture cards into your daily devotions. Once you have prayed, and listened to hear from the Holy Spirit, then you can read the encouraging scriptures aloud so that you will begin to memorize them. Lastly, meditate upon the scriptures to see if the Holy Spirit gives you a rhema word that becomes alive within your spirit. This will infuse and empower you for the journey as well.

After consistently executing the encouraging scripture plan of action, you should see significant results. Of course, consistency is very important. Ask yourself, "How bad do I want to reach this goal? How much am I willing to sacrifice to reach my goal?" Be prepared to work hard and put in the time to achieve your goal. Working hard for something we don't care about is called stress. However, working hard for something we love is called passion. In many instances you may need to do what you have never done to get what you have never had. However, that does not mean that your goal is unachievable. Forge ahead when you are challenged. You are a work in progress. Don't give up before you see the manifestation of what God has called you to do. When you get overwhelmed, take a break and then regain your focus. Remain laser-focused on your vision so that you can see clearly where you are in the process. Keep your faith strong in God. Former heavyweight champion Mohammad Ali once said, *"I hated every minute of training, but I said **Don't quit**! Suffer now and live the rest of your life as a champion."* While you will not suffer when you continuously execute your plan of action, you will be the undisputed champion at winning over lack of motivation.

"Commit your way to the Lord and trust Him," as Psalm 37:5 encourages. Tell yourself, "Today I will focus on taking one step forward; no matter how small or large a step." Keep moving toward your goal. It is paramount that you believe when others doubt, work when others doubt, and work when others refuse. Continue when others quit, and you will win when others lose. **Believe in yourself**. After all, this is your goal. Refuse to listen to anyone who attempts to talk you out of reaching your goal because they have no goal, vision, or because they have given up on their dreams.

The next very important step that will help you reach your goal is to surround yourself with positive people. Surround yourself with dreamers and positive thinkers. But, most of all surround yourself with those who see greatness within you, even while you are pressing toward your goal of becoming motivated. It is much easier to accomplish a goal with those who have your best interest at heart and with those who aspire to reach the same goal.

I read an online article about Arianna Alexander who graduated high school with a 5.1 GPA on a 4.0 scale. Yes, that's right 5.1 and not your normal 4.0. This student was accepted into 26 colleges, including six Ivy League. The total scholarships were more than $3 million. What stuck out in my mind is the fact that she stated, *"I had a plan and I stuck to it. There were many obstacles in my way and quite frankly, there were times when even I did not think that I would make it. However, I reminded myself that I have people who love and support me no matter if I stumble or even fall a few times."*

Her dad encouraged her to apply for $3 million in scholarships because another student had already obtained $1 million. Each time she reached a goal, her dad would encourage her to move to a higher level until she reached the $3 million goal. This is an excellent example of surrounding yourself with those who support you, as well as surrounding yourself with an awesome cheerleading squad and those who will encourage you. Since you are aspiring to reach another level, the following inspirational reading will encourage you:

EVERYONE CAN'T SIT IN YOUR FRONT ROW
Author Unknown

Life is a theater so invite your audiences carefully. Not everyone is spiritually healthy and mature enough to have a FRONT ROW seat in our lives. There are some people in your life that need to be loved from a distance.

It's amazing what you can accomplish when you let go, or at least minimize your time with draining, negative, incompatible, not-going-anywhere relationships, friendships, fellowships and family! Observe the relationships around you. Pay attention to: Which ones lift, and which ones lean? Which ones encourage, and which ones discourage? Which ones are on a path of growth uphill and which ones are just going downhill? When you leave certain people, do you feel better or feel worse? Which ones always have drama or don't really understand, know and appreciate you and the gift that lies within you?

When you seek growth, peace of mind, love, and truth the easier it will become for you to decide WHO GETS TO SIT IN YOUR FRONT ROW, and who should be moved to the balcony of your life.

You cannot change the people **around you**…but you can change the people **you are around**! Ask God for wisdom and discernment and choose wisely the people who sit in the FRONT ROW of your life. Remember that FRONT ROW seats are for special and deserving people and those who sit in your FRONT ROW should be chosen carefully.

Your FRONT ROW is reserved for those who celebrate you and not just tolerate you. Your exclusive front row seating is reserved for those persons who are cheering you on, encouraging you to reach your fullest potential. It is absolutely amazing what you can accomplish when you let go, or at least minimize your time with energy drainers, joy stealers, not-going-anywhere relationships, friendships, and fellowship as noted in the inspirational poem. Behavior speaks, so pay close attention to those who don't clap when you win. Therefore, choose your audience and FRONT ROW very carefully. Surround yourself with your best cheerleaders. While you cannot change the people around you…you can change the people you are around. Never feel guilty once the Holy Spirit separates you from a relationship. It's perfectly fine to outgrow relationships. This does not mean that you can't treat them with respect. But it does mean that you should no longer spend time together with them as in the past.

> Behavior speaks. Therefore, pay close attention to those who do not clap when you win.

Keep moving as you press toward your goal, supported and encouraged by Ecclesiastes 3, which says that everything has a season.

[1] There is a season (a time appointed) for everything and a time for every delight and event or purpose under heaven—
[2] A time to be born and a time to die;
A time to plant and a time to uproot what is planted.
[3] A time to kill and a time to heal;
A time to tear down and a time to build up.
[4] A time to weep and a time to laugh;
A time to mourn and a time to dance.
[5] A time to throw away stones and a time to gather stones;
A time to embrace and a time to refrain from embracing.
[6] A time to search and a time to give up as lost;
A time to keep and a time to throw away.
[7] A time to tear apart and a time to sew together;
A time to keep silent and a time to speak.
[8] A time to love and a time to hate;
A time for war and a time for peace.
Ecclesiastes 3:1-8 AMP

Therefore, refuse to have a pity party once the Holy Spirit separates you from a relationship. Trust that He knows what it takes to get you to your expected end according to Jeremiah 29:11. So, rest assured that the Holy Spirit has your perfect flight plan from your Heavenly Father.

[11] For I know the thoughts that I think toward you, saith the Lord, thoughts of peace, and not of evil, to give you an expected end.
Jeremiah 29:11 KJV

¹¹ For I know the plans and thoughts that I have for you,' says the Lord, 'plans for peace and well-being and not for disaster to give you a future and a hope.
Jeremiah 29:11 AMP

And since the Holy Spirit is tasked with leading and guiding you into all truth and righteousness, He will gently "nudge" you or tug on your heart until you separate from that relationship you have outgrown. He knows when your audience and "front row" seating have changed. He knows when it is time to move some people from your "front row" to the "balcony" of your life. So be prepared to get your cell phone, if necessary, to scroll, select, and delete any negative influences that will deter you from reaching your goal. Be reminded that people come into our lives for our betterment or in some cases for our detriment. In many instances God sends people into our lives to help us reach our goals or destiny. You definitely need those cheering you on and supporting your goals in your inner circle. Your strong support system will be a positive part of your equation as you march toward victory by God's grace.

Another way to reach your goal of becoming more motivated is to enlist the help of an awesome certified life coach. Anyone who feels stuck in the maze of life can benefit from Christian Life Coaching. Many individuals have **hopes and dreams about how things could be better**. Other individuals have **energy and passion that appears to inspire the person, but also the energy drainers that pull the person down**. Some individuals have **attitudes and abilities that impact how they see potential for the future, but that might be squelched or frustrated in the present**. People have **routines, habits, and ways of doing things that might need to be**

changed. Good coaches **HEAR** what clients say by listening. As a change agent, your life coach will ask very focused questions. Experienced interviewers have learned the fine art of getting to core issues through focused questioning. They show that the skillful use of good questions is like the techniques of a brain surgeon: incisive, revealing, and powerful.

Thought-provoking questions are designed to make you think. This should enable your coach to discover things about you. These questions may also cause you to discover things about yourself. It is better for coaches to ask what, when, how, who, or where questions because they usually do not encourage analytical thinking, excuses, defensiveness, or trips to the past. However, it is noted that **why** questions facilitate analytical thinking, excuses, defensiveness and trips to the past. Your Christian life coach can utilize a spiritual toolkit which has several powerful tools inclusive of but not limited to the following:

➤ Bible—this is the most important tool for a Christian life coach. The Holy Spirit will lead and guide the coach in the right direction.

➤ A Spiritual magnifying glass will enlarge the picture when the coach needs more enlightenment.

➤ Spiritual magnets will attract and find the missing pieces of the coaching puzzle.

➤ Spiritual pliers will allow the coach to extract something from the client that may be blocking progress.

➢ Spiritual measuring tape will allow your coach to hold you accountable.

➢ Spiritual WD40 oil will help you loosen up if you get overwhelmed.

➢ A Spiritual mirror will take you back to see what can be changed.

In conclusion, remember that it is **your** decision to become more motivated. One of the most important steps to reach your goal is to **believe that you can**. The battlefield will always be in the mind. Don't allow anyone to talk you out of your goal. The noisome pestilence, the naysayers, and those sent to take you off course will always show up. However, when they show up always remind them that, *"I can do ALL things through Christ who strengthens me."* Tell the negative committee in your head to sit down and shut up. Be encouraged by Proverbs 18:21 which states that, *"Death and life are in the power of the tongue,"* and focus daily on speaking life. Sometimes you must verbalize what you are thinking. Look in the mirror and say *"I believe in myself; I believe that I am becoming more motivated, I have been equipped with all the necessary tools to reach my goal. God is not in the business of setting me up to fail. Therefore, I depend on Him to walk with me as I walk through this process. He has promised never to leave me nor forsake me. My faith is in GOD! I will cooperate with God's perfect plan for me and as I do, I will become more motivated each day."* Don't forget to utilize encouraging scriptures to help you reach your goal. Commit your way to the Lord and trust Him as Psalm 37:5 encourages:

Commit thy way unto the Lord; trust also in him; and he shall bring it to pass. KJV

Commit your way to the Lord; Trust in Him also and He will do it.
AMP

Surround yourself with positive people inclusive of dreamers, and those who see greatness within you, even while you are pressing toward your goal of becoming motivated. Remember that behavior speaks. Therefore, pay close attention. Amos 3:3 asks a very specific question below:

Can two walk together, except they be agreed? KJV

Do two men walk together unless they have made an appointment?
AMP

Stop trying to walk with people who are not equipped for **your** journey, because they are an unnecessary weight. Hebrews 12:1-2 reminds us not only to lay aside weights, but it tells us how this can be done (verse 2):

¹…let us lay aside every weight, and the sin which doth so easily beset us, and let us run with patience the race that is set before us, ² Looking unto Jesus the author and finisher of our faith. KJV

It may become necessary to enlist the help of a Certified Christian Life Coach to help you reach your goal. Most coaches have selected a specific niche and have concentrated on that area as their specialty. A certified coach has gone through rigorous training, passed exams and has been issued certifications from an institution, which endorses them. Please exercise your right to inquire about your potential coach's credentials. You should feel relieved that you have chosen a qualified professional to help you reach your goal.

Many times, people tend to enlist the help of ill-equipped friends, and associates to help them accomplish a task for which they are not qualified. Don't set yourself up for failure, and don't compromise your relationship in this manner. Coaches who are experienced interviewers have learned the fine art of getting to core issues through focused questioning. Since thought-provoking questions have the propensity to make people think, you may discover things about yourself.

I feel the need to remind you of a very important term known as "self-talk" that can delay your arrival at your targeted goal. If you are like most people, you have daily inner conversations with yourself. According to www.psychologydictionary.org self-talk is defined as: *the dialogue that we have with ourselves that can confirm and <u>reinforce</u> both positive and <u>negative</u> beliefs*. Athletes are trained to use positive cues to keep them focused on their goals. I will hasten to say that in your case we are referring to <u>positive</u> beliefs and self-talk that will help you accomplish your goal. Positive self-talk is an excellent tool to use for skill development and skill execution. Therefore, you can adopt this technique to help you reach your goal. Occasionally you may need to refocus your self-talk. We all use self-talk throughout the day. The way you talk to yourself can increase or decrease your stress. Learn to identify your negative mental and emotional self-talk triggers. When you begin to experience the self-talk stress triggers, verbally challenge and dispute your thinking errors; put the stress and situation in proper perspective; take time to problem solve, and lastly, find a positive or God-centered thought or image that you can substitute for the negative self-talk.

Lastly, your Christian life coach may also pray with you and listen to the Holy Spirit regarding a specific concern for which you are seeking assistance. **You can do it! Let's gooooooo!**

HOW TO BE MORE CONFIDENT
1. Don't Compare; focus on you.
2. Relax, don't sweat the small stuff.
3. Love yourself, you are a gift, nothing would be the same if you didn't exist.
4. Be positive and look for the good in every situation.
5. Don't beat yourself up if you stumble; pick yourself up, dust yourself off, and get back into the race.

CHAPTER ONE REFLECTIONS

➢ List five ways you can be more confident:

_____
_____
_____
_____
_____

➢ List the first step toward getting motivated to achieve your goal:

_____
_____
_____
_____
_____

➢ List the other suggested steps toward getting motivated to achieve your goal:

_____
_____
_____
_____
_____

➢ Explain the components of a Christian life coach's spiritual toolkit:

_____
_____
_____
_____
_____

➢ List those persons who should sit in your FRONT ROW:

_____
_____
_____
_____
_____

➢ Define positive self-talk and discuss its importance toward reaching your goal:

_____
_____
_____
_____
_____

➢ What are the most salient points you've gleaned from this chapter?

_____
_____
_____
_____
_____
_____
_____
_____

➢ How should we respond when the Holy Spirit separates us from a relationship? List the supporting scripture.

_____
_____
_____

➤ Explain the fine art Christian coaches have accomplished as interviewers.

➤ Share how Philippians 4:13 has empowered you to continue to press toward your goal?

PERSONAL NOTES

Chapter Two
Set S.M.A.R.T. Goals

A goal without a plan is just a wish.

I am reminded of the adage, *"How do you eat an elephant?"* Of course, the answer is, *"One bite at a time."* Now that you have a specific mission to accomplish, and the methodology, it is time to set some goals. These goals will ensure that you stay focused as you walk through your process. Every large goal is made-up of smaller parts, which makes it much easier, more fun, and exciting in many instances (as you check off the smaller goals in route to your larger goal). Sometimes these smaller parts are different facets of a bigger goal, and sometimes they are simply identical, measured increments of the big goal. Therefore, your smaller goals or clear steps can be carried out initially or repeated as the need arises.

Usually setting S.M.A.R.T. goals is invaluable in helping to accomplish your mission. Goals can be broken down into smaller sizes which are more manageable. Therefore, we will take the first letter of S.M.A.R.T. which is the **S** that represents **specific.** You have chosen to become more motivated as your specific goal. Since a picture is usually worth a thousand words, and Habakkuk encourages you to write the vision—write your goal and incorporate it onto a vision board.

[2]Write the vision, and make it plain upon tables, that he may run that readeth it. [3]For the vision is yet for an appointed time, but at

the end it shall speak, and not lie: though it tarry, wait for it; because it will surely come, it will not tarry. Habakkuk 2:2-3 KJV

In addition to the vision board, you may include scripture reading and positive self-talk mentioned in Chapter One. Look in the mirror several times a day and repeat positive affirmations. You may read the encouraging scriptures in **Appendix C**, or you may place encouraging scriptures on your refrigerator, bathroom mirror, and computer. Let nothing or no one deter you from your daily regimen of speaking and reading these positive scriptures. Repetition will allow you to reach your goal. Before long, you will notice that you are memorizing these scriptures. However, it is still very important to speak them. Remember that Romans 10:17 tells us that faith comes by hearing.

[17] So then faith cometh by hearing and hearing by the word of God.
Romans 10:17 KJV

Though I am not a grammarian, I do know that hearing is a gerund which ends in **"ing."** Therefore, hearing is an ongoing process. So, you must hear your positive scriptures daily, because your faith will not come from having heard in the past, but rather it will come from your daily speaking these encouraging scriptures. You are not in a competition, so you will not need to feel unnecessary pressure, or stress because of competition. Run your race and focus on your prize of becoming motivated in the timeframe that you will set for reaching your goal.

These are some **specific** things that you will do to help you become more motivated. Remember that in order to achieve success you must have the determination and the will. In other words, it will not happen by the process of osmosis. You must put in the work to reach your goal. Daily remind yourself that this is your goal, and no one can do it for you. This is your decision, and **YOU CAN DO IT**! There is no elevator to success, so be prepared to take the stairs one at a time, focused on the fact that every journey begins one step at a time. Also focus on the fact that every expert was once a novice. Once you reach your goal you can look back and embrace your tenacity while you thank God for blessing you to accomplish the goal.

> *There is no elevator to success so be prepared to take the stairs one at a time.*

I am reminded of a children's book entitled, *"The Little Engine That Could."* In the tale, a long train must be pulled over a high mountain. For various reasons larger engines refuse to pull the train. No worries, because the request is sent to a small engine, who agrees to try. The small engine succeeds in pulling the train over the mountain while repeating its motto: *"I think I can."*

The story of the little engine has been told and retold for years. The underlying theme is the same — a stranded train is unable to find an engine willing to take it on over difficult terrain to its destination. Only the little blue engine is willing to try and, while repeating, *"I think I can, I think I can,"* overcomes a seemingly impossible task. You are embarking upon a similar regimen while you adopt a positive attitude by saying, **"I KNOW I CAN DO IT!"**

You will find yourself moving progressively faster from one step to the next as you get closer to obtaining the goal. Remember to reward yourself for the small steps you accomplish in route to your big goal. Once you have formed a habit of speaking life to your goal by repeating positive scriptures, after a period of about six months you may want to treat yourself. Your reward system serves as a reminder that you are reaching your goal one step at a time. Your reward system will also give you an energy boost which will enable you to continue to press toward your goal.

Next, we will take the second letter of S.M.A.R.T. which is the **M** that represents **measurable.** Keep in mind that you have chosen to become more motivated as you move towards your specific goal. In order to resist becoming overwhelmed by the big picture, your goal must be measurable. Ask yourself, *"How long do I need to reach this goal without being stressed?"* Your answer will provide you with a reasonably measurable plan to march toward your goal. Whether it is nine months or a year, you will be able to measure your progress.

Our first unit of measurement is **behavior**. Motivation enables goal-directed behavior and is evidenced through action. Measures such as speed, performance, or persistence exerted can also be measured. Once you see yourself moving closer and performing more consistently your level of excitement begins to move higher up the scale. Therefore, you will be excited and ready to pursue your regimen to reach your goal. You will be eager to press on.

The second unit of measurement is **speed**. In many instances, motivation can manifest itself in terms of the amount of time it takes a person to reach his or her goal. As a Board-Certified Temperament Therapist, I personally know that it can usually take people with a melancholy temperament a lot longer to reach their goal because of their tendency to procrastinate. Therefore, those with melancholy tendencies may need more coaxing, encouragement and self-talk than people with the choleric temperament who are usually self-motivated, confident leaders. The person with the sanguine temperament is usually inspiring to others and usually enthusiastic. None of the temperaments should have worries because as God's children they are overcomers. We know that a winner never quits, and a quitter never wins. So, if you are aware that you have melancholy tendencies and you aspire to become self-motivated or just more motivated, you may want to partner with a friend who has sanguine or choleric tendencies to help you reach your goal. Keep in mind that commitment and action are key components.

The third unit of measurement is **choice**. Yes, a choice can indicate one's level of motivation and motivation determines what you do. Specifically, when you choose between conflicting goals such as, *"Should I repeat my encouraging scriptures today or should I just hang out with friends?"* We can say that your motivation for the chosen goal of hanging out will win out instead of your planned goal of reading encouraging scriptures. Of course, this is not how you reach your goal. So, try to be like the postage stamp which sticks with the letter until it reaches its destination.

> Motivation determines what you do!

The fourth unit of measurement is a **test**. Remember you were asked to take a pre-motivation test to see exactly where you started on the spectrum. After you have completed your goal timeline you will then take a post-motivation test. You can see the progress made during your journey. You will have the opportunity to see your improvement from beginning to end. Tests are usually an excellent measuring tool to chart progress whether it is in school, at work, or in your case on a personal journey of becoming motivated. Nothing is more satisfying, in my opinion, than being able to see where I started and review my progress as a final product to chart my speed, and rate of improvement. What a sense of fulfillment! You can experience Dr. Abraham Maslow's self–actualization listed at the top of the Hierarchy of Human needs defined as a person's motivation to reach his or her full potential.

The fifth unit of measure is **body language**. Body language is a form of non-verbal communication involving the use of stylized gestures, postures, and physiological signs which act as cues to other people. Humans unconsciously send and receive non-verbal signals through body language. It is safe to say that most persons who are not motivated present in a lackadaisical manner. It is not easy for them to look you in the eye. The impact of your message is affected by the amount of eye contact you maintain with the person to whom you are speaking with. One who makes eye contact is normally perceived as more favorable and confident. Find comfortable sitting and standing postures that work for you; avoid any rigid or slouching positions. Persons who are not motivated may eventually begin to separate themselves from groups and socialize less because of their low self-esteem and lack of motivation. Even when they are in the presence of a positive person their shoulders may drop, or their eyes may wander, and they may speak with uncertainty such as, *"Um, Ah Oh well"*, or *whatever."* However, a person who is confident and motivated uses positive gestures, expressions, tone of voice, good eye contact, uncrossed arms, and they may lean toward the speaker.

During your journey many may have said that you would never reach your goal. Others may have said it was not worth it. But at the end of the day you get to hold your head up high, stick your chest out, and declare yourself a winner. Late South African President, Nelson Mandela, is quoted as saying, *"It always seems impossible until it is done."* Your journey will reveal hidden strength you never realized you had until you put it to the test. It is very important to remember that you can hope something will happen, believe something will happen or take courage and make something happen. You chose big, bad, bold faith, to make something happen. Congratulations on your excellent choice!

Next, we will take the third letter of S.M.A.R.T. which is the **A** that represents **attainable.** You must ask yourself if you are setting an attainable goal. Your answer should be based upon your character traits, and in some cases temperament tendencies, and even learned behavior. The melancholy temperament as mentioned earlier has a tendency to procrastinate. Therefore, if you set a short-term goal and do not work on it consistently, you will need to partner with the choleric temperament to help pace you to your goal. The choleric temperament is usually self-motivated, a great leader and organizer, and an excellent motivator. And if that is not enough, the choleric is usually confident. They will cheer you on during your journey and meet you at the finish line with a cheering squad!

Webster defines character as one of the attributes or features that make up and distinguish an individual. Dr. Richard G. and Dr. Phyllis J. Arno define temperament as the inborn part of man that determines how he or she reacts with people, places, or things. When God assigned our destiny, He provided everything that we would need to fulfill our preordained purpose before we left His assembly line. Therefore, He knew what character traits, as well as temperament tendencies to give each of us. However, we must tap into God's plan for our lives to see where we will reach our fullest potential. Rest assured that He has no plans for us to fail because that would not bring Him glory.

Therefore, before you set your attainable goal, take into consideration your character traits, temperament tendencies, learned behavior, character, birth order, and growth in the Lord. This assessment will save you a lot of time and you should avoid the trap of setting an unrealistic goal. Unrealistic goals can cause your stress level to unnecessarily increase. So, armed with the knowledge of what should work best for you after taking your assessment, you are now ready to set your best possible attainable goal. Will you need a six-month, nine month or a one-year goal? You determine what works best. Please be as honest as you can with yourself. You know yourself; think carefully before you make this very important decision. After all you will begin working toward this goal. If you have not established an attainable goal, you are only setting yourself up for failure. Initially you may feel uncertain or unsure about undertaking a new project. However, this feeling should subside once you continuously focus on your encouraging scriptures (continue to speak them out loud daily); pray, and trust God. You may also contact me to enroll in my amazing, ***Don't Quit Master Class*** that will provide very specific information to help you set and reach your S.M.A.R.T. goals within a reasonable timeframe. There is also an option for me to serve as your accountability partner. Continue to press toward the goal as Paul did in Philippians 3:13-14:

> [13]*Brothers and sisters, I do not consider that I have made it my own yet; but one thing I do: forgetting what lies behind and reaching forward to what lies ahead,* [14] *I press on toward the goal to win the [heavenly] prize of the upward call of God in Christ Jesus. AMP*

I am reminded that I quit high school multiple times in the 10th, 11th, and 12th grades. BUT GOD had a plan for my life. I was not satisfied. I knew there was more to life than what I was living. But how was I ever to reach my destiny without a high school diploma and a higher education? By the grace of God, I graduated number 18 out of 322 students in my class. Once I decided to go forth, I sat down with an action plan and began to set strategic educational goals. All praise, glory and honor to God, today both my husband and I have earned Doctor of Philosophy degrees. We both graduated Summa Cum Laude only by God's grace. Pardon me while I shout, "Hallelujah!"

Our journey was **NEVER** easy, but we achieved our educational goals because we persevered and continued to call those things that be not as though they were. And, yes, we put the time in and did our share of hard work. On the following page I have shared one of my favorite motivational poems entitled ***"Don't Quit"*** that will help you focus and keep it moving. The day that you finally reach your goal you will be so happy that you included this poem as a part of your daily regimen.

DON'T QUIT

Variation of "Don't Quit" original poem by poet, John Greenleaf Whittier (1807-1892)

When things go wrong, as they sometimes will,
When the road you're trudging seems all uphill,
When the funds are low and the debts are high,
And you want to smile but you have to sigh,
When care is pressing you down a bit—
Rest if you must, but don't you quit.

Life is odd with its twists and turns,
As everyone sometimes learns.
And many a person turns about
When an individual might have won
had he or she stuck it out.
Don't give up though the pace seems slow—
You may succeed with yet another blow.

Often the goal is nearer than it seems
To a faint and faltering woman or man;
Often the struggler has given up
When he or she might have captured the victor's cup;
And one learned too late when the night came down,
How close he or she was to the golden crown.

Success is failure turned inside out—
The silver tint of the clouds of doubt,
And when you never can tell how close you are,
It may be near when it seems afar;

> So stick to the fight when you're hardest hit—
> It's when things seem worst, you mustn't quit.

Next, we will take the fourth letter of S.M.A.R.T. which is the **R** that represents **reasonable or realistic**. Ask yourself if you have all the things you need to complete your goal. Have you talked with your cheering squad? The following questions should be considered prior to setting your goal:

- Have you separated yourself from those who may not have your best interest at heart?

- Have you selected your encouraging scriptures to repeat daily?

- Have you posted your encouraging scriptures on your refrigerator, computer and other places where you can't miss them?

- Have you researched information that will help you hire a Christian life coach if necessary?

- Have you posted your scripture/quotes on a vision board? Write the vision according to Habakkuk 2:2-3.

- Have you visited **www.drmaryjhuntley** to enroll in the *Don't Quit Master Class,* if necessary?

- Have you factored in your temperament tendencies, characteristics, learned behavior, and character?

Answering these questions can alleviate stress and self-sabotage efforts. It is imperative that you are brutally honest before you answer these questions and ensure that you are setting realistic goals. Your goal should also stretch you beyond your normal capacity. It should also be so exciting that it must motivate you to achieve it, but not so big or complex that you will lose the will to accomplish it. Please remember to avoid the following at all cost according to www.smart-goal-guide.com:

MISTAKES YOU MUST AVOID

- You think goals are something you only do once a year—at New Year.

- You set New Year's goals, but you don't achieve them. Without realizing it you build up the belief that you are not good at achieving goals.

- You don't spend enough time taking stock of how your life currently is so that you can be clear on what you would prefer instead.

- You don't take enough time to think about what it is you really, really want.

- You have too many goals.

- You don't put your goals into writing.

- You don't think through the specific metrics of your goal – i.e. your goal is too general.

- Your goal is far too big for you to achieve. You have not broken it down into smaller, more manageable goals.

- The goal is outside your control and influence – you could never make it happen on your own.

- Your goal is a 'should' goal and not a 'want' goal.

- You don't know 'why' you want your goal.

- You don't spend enough time working out the possible downsides to achieving your goal.

- You don't have a plan, an effective course of action.

- You don't take enough action.

- You don't think through, or find, the resources that you need to achieve your goal.

- You don't go where you need to go, contact who you need to contact, or get what you need to get.

- You don't develop the skills you need.

- You don't believe: *"This is Possible,"* *"I want to do this,"* *"I can do this,"*- the three core beliefs behind setting goals and achieving them.

- You have a clash of values. For example, security is more important to you than risk, and yet you set a goal that requires high risk.

- You are just not the kind of person to achieve the kind of goal you set.

Persistence is very important here. If you don't achieve your goal of repeating as many encouraging scriptures in a given day, don't have a pity party. Simply be grateful that you have started your goal and press harder during the days ahead. Never feel pressured into setting a realistic goal because that will only cause unnecessary stress and frustration.

Always remember that a winner never quits, and a quitter never wins. So, keep marching toward your goal because you **can** do it.

> A winner never quits, and a quitter never wins!

Next, we will take the fifth and final letter of S.M.A.R.T. which is the **T** that represents **time**. Ask yourself if you have all the things you need to complete your goal inclusive of a definite timeframe or timeline. Time management is very important. A goal must have a deadline. This will provide you with the necessary focus and sense of urgency (and in some cases excitement) to make it happen. When you finalize your specific goal sentence and write it down, it must include your deadline. Ask yourself when do I want to have my goal achieved or completed? Your realistic date should be incorporated into your goal statement so that you have a measurable tool for goal accomplishment. Consider the following questions before setting your timeline:

- ➢ Have you attached an achievable timeline that takes into consideration your temperament tendency discussed earlier?

- ➢ Do you believe that you can do this? Has your cheering squad committed to support you for the duration of the journey?

➤ Have you written an action plan or a goal worksheet? Have you done all the necessary research or homework to ensure that you will set a realistic timeline and reach your goal? **Avoid time wasters and distractions.**

The Urgent/Important Matrix

Great time management means being effective as well as efficient. Managing time effectively, and achieving the things that you want to achieve, means spending your time on things that are important and not just urgent. To do this, you need to distinguish clearly between what is urgent and what is important:

Urgent: These activities demand immediate attention but are often associated with someone else's goals rather than our own.

Important: These are activities that lead to achieving your goals and have the greatest impact on your life.

This concept, coined the Eisenhower Principle, is said to be how former President Dwight Eisenhower organized his tasks. It was rediscovered and brought into the mainstream as the Urgent/Important Matrix by Stephen Covey in his 1994 business classic, *The Seven Habits of Highly Effective People*. The Urgent/Important Matrix is a powerful way of organizing tasks based on priorities. Using it helps you overcome the natural tendency to focus on urgent activities, so that you can have time to focus on what's truly important.

Urgent and Important: Activities in this area relate to dealing with critical issues as they arise and meeting significant commitments. Perform these duties now.

Important, But Not Urgent: *These success-oriented tasks are critical to achieving goals.* Plan to do these tasks next.

Urgent, But Not Important: These chores do not move you forward toward your own goals. Manage by delaying them, cutting them short, and rejecting requests from others. Postpone these chores.

Not Urgent and Not Important: These trivial interruptions are just a distraction and should be avoided if possible. However, be careful not to mislabel things like time with family and recreational activities as not important. *Avoid these distractions!*

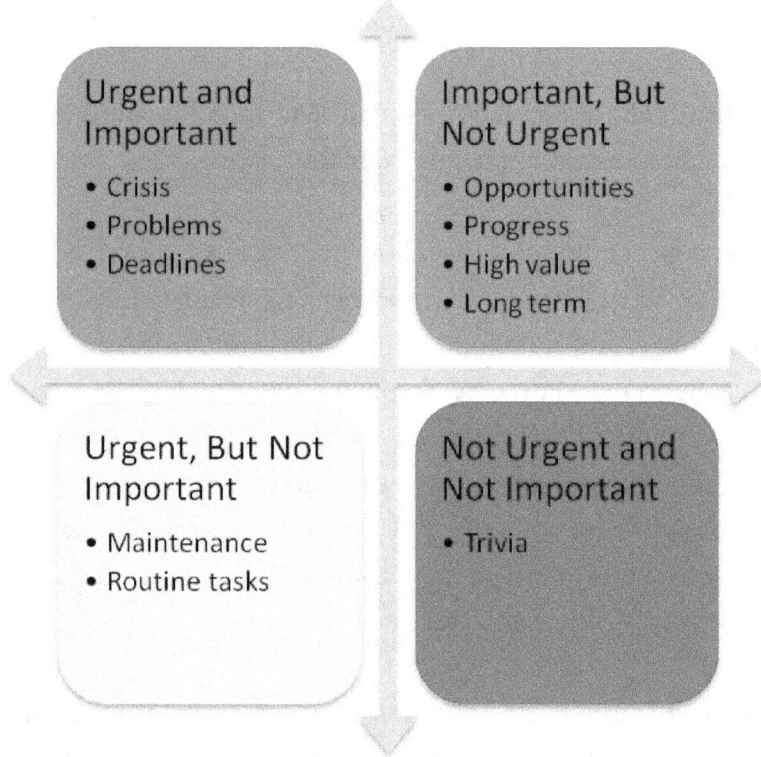

Used with permission from Corporate Training Materials

Suffice it to say that you may have had a few challenges, hiccups or bumps in the road, but your cheering squad is seated in your "front row" to celebrate you and to cheer you on to your goal. They were there for you through some very challenging times. You celebrated the steps of progress since the beginning of your journey. As you continue you can utilize this very important information for reaching other goals. In fact, utilizing the S.M.A.R.T. goal technique will ensure that you continue to complete your goals in a timely manner. I will go a step further to say that you have gleaned helpful information that will enhance your goal setting technique and ability. No matter what size the goal, you are now equipped to handle it.

So, now that we have the basics, you should feel a sense of accomplishment and fulfillment since you began the journey to get motivated to reach your goal. It is wonderful to know that you can move on to the next thing that you have aspired to do but just did not have the motivation to attempt it. Now, armed with this information, you can simply start the process over again to tackle your life goals of education, finance, health and wellness or whatever you set out to do. This action of setting S.M.A.R.T. goals will help you reach the finish line as you are declared the winner.

CHAPTER TWO REFLECTIONS

➤ Explain each letter in S.M.A.R.T. goals:

➢ List units of measurement to help achieve your goal:

_____
_____
_____
_____
_____

➢ Describe the body language used by a confident person:

_____
_____
_____
_____
_____
_____
_____
_____
_____

➢ List **specific** things you can do to achieve your goal to become more motivated:

_____
_____
_____
_____
_____
_____
_____
_____
_____
_____
_____
_____

➢ Explain why you should write your goals and list supporting scripture (s):

___

➢ Describe the best way to reach a "large" goal:

___

➢ What is the best way to eat an elephant?

PERSONAL NOTES

Dr. Mary's Motivational Doses
(Meditate Upon One Daily)

A quitter **NEVER** wins, and a winner **NEVER** quits. Constantly remind yourself that you CAN do this, you were made for this.

Where **GOD** guides, He provides. *"But my God shall supply ALL of your need according to your riches in glory by Christ Jesus."* (Philippians 4:19)

Allow **FAITH** to answer when fear knocks. Fear is a bully that comes to take you off the course of your purpose. Allow **FAITH** to handle your business for you. (Hebrew 11:6)

Push past pain to purpose. Pain is an indicator that you are about to give birth.

You're an eagle, soar above the storm.

Mediocrity is not acceptable in pursuit of excellence. Don't hang out with it during your pursuit of excellence.

Don't panic it's just a test. You can't even spell testimony without the word test. So, pass the test and keep it moving.

Live your best life today! God came that we might have an abundant life not a life of barely making it. (St. John 10:10)

Some connections provide fuel, others drain your energy. Ensure that those connected to you are providing fuel and not serving as a drain to deplete your energy.

To win you must first begin. Don't allow fear to paralyze you.

Every expert was once a novice. All of us began somewhere.

Eat an elephant one bite at a time. Don't allow the big picture to overwhelm you. Divide goals into "bite-size" pieces (one at a time).

See the big picture. If you find yourself about to get frustrated imagine the finished product, and the fulfillment it will bring.

Press toward the goal. Keep it moving until you have reached your goal. (Philippians 4:13)

Proper preparation prevents poor performance. This will allow you to perform in an excellent manner.

Never give up on yourself or your dreams. Joseph went from the pit to the palace. (Genesis 41:1-57)

Celebrating small victories can motivate you to finish strong.

Make changes not excuses.

You are more than a conqueror. (Romans 8:37)

Speak Life. Know your worth!

Tell the negative committee that meets inside your head to sit down and shut up.

I've seen too many victories to let defeat have the last word.

Rock bottom will teach you lessons that the mountain tops never will.

Where GOD guides, He provides.

Choose faith over fear. Visit the Hallmarks of Faith in Hebrews 11 to see the great works that were accomplished.

Fear will not decide my future. God clearly knew us because He made us. He has not given you a spirit of fear (2 Timothy 1:7)

Chapter Three
Do What You Love

PURPOSE— "Until purpose is discovered existence has no meaning." Dr. Myles Munroe

Now that you have set your S.M.A.R.T. goal and become motivated, it is time to focus on what you love. This may not be the easiest thing to do, especially if you find yourself performing several tasks throughout the day. If you are unsure of what you love, ask yourself the following questions:

➤ If I had a choice of doing one thing for the rest of my life, what would that be?

➤ What did I enjoy doing in my childhood?

➤ What activity makes me feel like I am in my zone?

➤ What am I doing when I feel like I'm in my "sweet spot?"

➤ What activity do I love so much until I would do it even if I did not get paid?

➤ What activity provides such a sense of fulfillment until time gets away very quickly because I am enjoying myself?

➤ What is the one activity I dreamed about, but never took time to attempt?

➢ What is my hobby?

Though you are asking different questions, you should see the same answer to some of the questions. This will be an indicator about what you love. Look closely at your answers. You will have a starting point to determine what you love. One of the best ways to determine what you love to do is to seek God through prayer and fasting. Since He created you in His image and likeness, surely, He knows exactly what problem He created you to solve before you left His assembly line. Not only does He know the problem He created you to solve, but He also gave you every ingredient that you would need to fulfill your purpose and assignment. Therefore, you can ask Him the specific purpose He had in mind when He created you. As you begin the process of fasting and praying and seeking God for the answer to your specific purpose, you will also notice that you develop a more intimate relationship with Him. You will be more cognizant and alert to His voice when He speaks. Therefore, you will know when He reveals what you were created to do. When God created you, He had a specific purpose in mind.

According to Dr. Myles Munroe *"Purpose is the original intent in the mind of the creator that motivated him to create a particular item. It is the why that explains the reason for existence. "Every product is the child of purpose. Until purpose is discovered, existence has no meaning."*

> **Dr. Myles Munroe says "Purpose is...**
> ...the original intent for the creation of a thing,
> ...the original reason for the existence of a thing;
> ...the end for which the means exist;
> ...the cause for the creation of a thing;
> ...the desired result that initiated production;
> ...the need that makes a manufacturer produce a specific product;
> ...the destination that prompts the journey;
> ...the expectation of the source;
> ...the objective for the subject;
> ...the aspiration for the inspiration, and
> ...the object one wills or resolves to have."

That explains why millions are walking around every day frustrated and unfulfilled. **Life simply has no meaning for them because they have not discovered their purpose.** Therefore, it is very important to discover one's purpose to help provide the fulfillment God has created each of us to experience.

Remember, God created you and me to solve a specific problem in the earth realm. And until we discover our purpose, we may go through life simply existing and not thriving and experiencing fulfillment. **So, pay close attention to those things that annoy you**. Could that be a part of your purpose? Could it be a problem you were created to solve?

Another method to discovering your purpose that will help you do what you love is to determine your strengths and your weaknesses. This can be determined by your motivational gifts. There are some things that you are just gifted and graced to do. In fact, when you operate in your gifting you operate like a well-oiled machine. Your gift looks so good on you and it provides a tremendous sense of fulfillment. What is the one thing that you were afraid to attempt because you felt that you would fail? You felt that you were just not good enough to succeed if you attempted it. However, you may have noticed that because you did not step up to the plate to attempt to flow in your gifting, the urge or unction never left you. Deep within you thought about how you could perform only if you were motivated and confident enough. Allow me to share a secret found in Romans 11:29, *"for God's gifts and his call are irrevocable."* (NIV)

Simply put, God placed within you at least one gift to bring Him glory. Just because you were not aware of the gift, or you were afraid to use your gift, He never changed His mind. He waited for you to realize that once you discovered your gift, you would never work another day in your life. You see your gift will make room for you and bring God all glory. You will not be totally fulfilled unless you are serving your gift in the area where you are assigned. If you are an exhorter, you must encourage others to aspire to reach their goals and feel good about themselves. If you are an apostle, you are honored to help others set up churches like the Apostle Paul did. If you are a teacher, you are quite satisfied teaching God's Word, so that others may apply it to their lives. And, if you are a preacher, you share God's word so that it may be used to change lives daily.

So, after asking yourself what is the one thing that would bring you fulfillment, focus on your answer. Take time to reflect upon your motivational gift(s) as described in Romans 12:6-8 below:

[6]We have different gifts, according to the grace given to each of us. If your gift is prophesying, then prophesy in accordance with your faith;

> *⁷ if it is serving, then serve; if it is teaching then teach;*
>
> *⁸ if it is to encourage, then give encouragement; if it is giving, then give generously; if it is to lead, do it diligently; if it is to show mercy, do it cheerfully. (NIV)*

There are various ways to discover your **spiritual gift**. First pray and make your request known to God. Then begin serving in a ministry that attracts you after you have observed for a period. As you serve, you will discover that you enjoy doing some things more than others. Pay close attention to your level of excitement, as well as how you are motivated when you serve. Does this ministry bring you a sense of fulfillment or does it deplete your energy? When you serve your gift in a certain ministry at church God will allow others to see how you are "graced" to serve. Often others will comment on how much your ministry blessed them. You will serve seemingly effortlessly to bring God all praise, glory and honor. Oftentimes those who are not graced to serve as well as you in a certain ministry will become irritated or annoyed. They will definitely not serve as effortlessly as you. Another way to determine your spiritual gift is to ask yourself what is the one thing that annoys you the most when you are at church? Is it because you feel that the church is run poorly? If so, there is a strong possibility that you have the gift of administration. Is it because you think that the poor and the needy are going neglected? If so, maybe you have the gift of mercy. Think about it while you reminisce and meditate upon Romans 12:6-8. Or you can take one of several spiritual gift tests administered and discuss the results with the test administrator. So, start your process of discovering your spiritual gift as soon as you can, so that you can do what you love in a spirit of excellence.

Once you discover your gift you will begin to serve with confidence and experience an awesome sense of fulfillment like never before. You may even ask yourself what took me so long to discover this awesome gift. However, be reminded of the adage, *"better late than never."* At least you have discovered a very important missing link to your destiny and an important piece to your success story. You are well on the way to enjoying freedom from procrastination, and lack of motivation. You have tapped into a very important source that will determine how you continuously *"do what you love."* After all life is meant to be enjoyed, and yes, we will have challenges along the way. God never intended for anyone to be miserable, unaware of their spiritual gift(s), and unfulfilled. In other words, God did not plan for His children to be broke, busted and disgusted. That is why He left us the Bible as the anecdote. Tap into this powerful Word to ensure that you maximize your ability and your happiness. One very important fact is that your calling is what you were made for and your vocation is what you are paid for.

Hypothetically, let's say that your spiritual gift is exhortation, which is also known as encouragement. Exhorters are also known as encouragers and influencers. They are relationship-driven to minister directly to people with hope and optimism. They offer positive influence while promoting discipleship. They constantly help others fulfill their destiny. Encouragers will usually have an encouraging word and motivate others when they are challenged to quit. They are usually very supportive and trustworthy. Those with the gift of exhortation usually serve very well as counselors, coaches, mentors, influencers, team builders, worship leaders, intercessory prayer leaders, and member care leaders. We need exhorters who will come alongside individuals and urge them to continue to reach their goal. The encourager and exhorter serve as great motivators in the body of Christ.

Therefore, to fulfill your preordained purpose, stay in your lane and do what you love. This will be far less stressful than trying to fit in someplace that does not satisfy your need. I have read several stories about successful corporate executives who resigned their positions to fulfill the call of God in their lives.

The joy the corporate executives experienced after leaving their corporate positions was phenomenal. They were less frustrated, experienced less stress, and were much happier and fulfilled. There is a significant difference when you do what you love. It will not feel like a job, but it will feel more like a hobby. You will fulfill this assignment in many instances without compensation because you love it. And equally important, you will be happy.

I have had the distinct honor and privilege of meeting several executive women leaders who are impacting the world in a phenomenal manner. They were gainfully employed in various organizations and corporations. However, despite the monetary rewards something was missing. They were not totally fulfilled, nor were they walking in their preordained purpose. There was much more to life for these phenomenal, trailblazers. Therefore, they decided to take a leap of faith in search of their pre-ordained purpose. They left the corporate world, government agency or private sector to satisfy the deep desire or need to feel fulfilled.

Though their decision to depart from a routine for many years was not easy, it was worth taking a chance. And because they believed in themselves, they continue to reap awesome benefits. After all, in order to get what you have never had you must do what you have never done. Since taking a leap of faith these phenomenal women have started amazing businesses providing the same products and services. However, there is a pivotal difference now. They have become entrepreneurs connecting with other awesome women in their areas of expertise to build dynamic empires. They continue to reach out to those of like minds to sharpen each other and keep each other abreast of the trends and changes that impact their business decisions.

There is no explanation for the fulfillment you feel when you are making boss moves, sharing your gift with others as you equip and empower them to impact the nation. That is awesome! There is nothing like sitting at the table with other executives strategizing business moves for your company instead of making strategic moves for another person's company. Many of these executives have built an awesome clientele throughout the United States. **They walked away from a definitive paycheck in order to fill an inner void known as purpose and indicated as self-actualization on Maslow's Hierarchy of Human Needs Chart Below**.

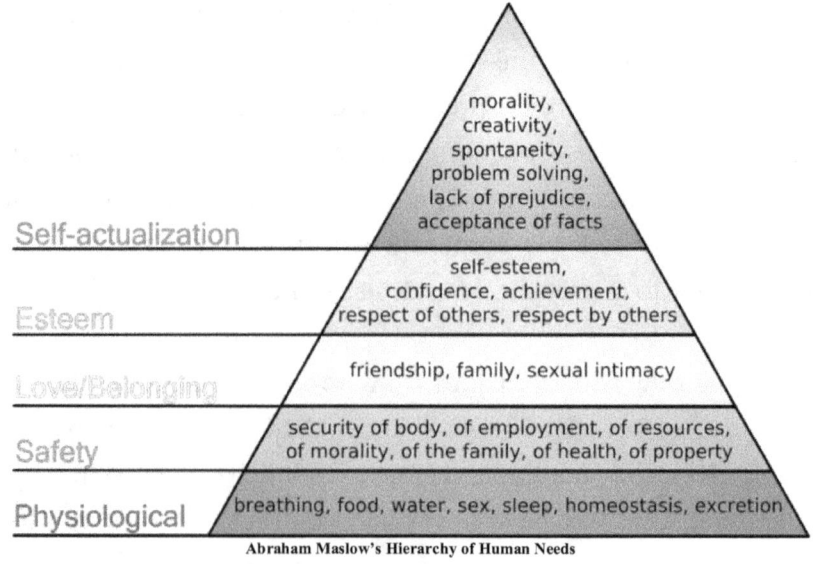

Abraham Maslow's Hierarchy of Human Needs

At the very peak of Maslow's hierarchy are the self-actualization needs. *"What a man can be, he must be,"* Maslow explained, referring to the need people must achieve for their full potential as humans. These executives sought to fulfill their preordained purpose, and they are growing by leaps and bounds. They are fulfilled doing what they love.

It wasn't until these executives started their own businesses and began contracting with organizations, teaching workshops and seminars, speaking on various platforms, hosting conferences and coaching sessions that they felt such a great sense of achievement, accomplishment, and fulfillment. Some even travel internationally to do what they love to do. When we do what we love to do time seems not to really matter, because we are fulfilled. When we do what we love it is usually a win-win situation—you and the audience you are serving have a phenomenal sense of accomplishment. And it doesn't get much better than that.

As a result of these executives pouring into their mentees and audiences, the mentees are exposed to wonderful opportunities that will allow them to grow and impact others. What a rewarding experience. Mentors and mentees are experiencing some of the most fulfilling times of their lives. What would have happened had these executives decided not to leave their comfort zones? These executives decided to do what they love. They took a huge leap of faith which rewarded them tremendously. And yes, they are globally impacting the world.

Are you doing what you love or are you satisfied in your comfort zone? Are you in that place where you are fulfilled after serving your gift and empowering others? If you are not experiencing a sense of fulfillment, you can. No, it may not be easy, but it is definitely possible. You are worth it, so take the risk. Do it for yourself. There is no need to continue down the path knowing that the benefits will be the same. Ask yourself, *"How bad do I want to feel fulfilled and accomplished?"* This is one of the most important questions to answer. It is my prayer that you take a leap of faith—do what you love.

CHAPTER THREE REFLECTIONS

➤ What questions can you ask to discover what you love?

➢ What does Dr. Munroe say about purpose?

___

➢ How can one discover his/her spiritual gift?

___

➤ Which scripture describes motivational gifts?

➤ Describe Maslow's Hierarchy of Human Needs.

PERSONAL NOTES

Chapter Four
Stay in Your Lane

Stay single-eyed, focused on your goal, serve where you are assigned.

Once you have discovered what brings you fulfillment and satisfaction, it is imperative that you stay focused and not deviate. Once you discover what you love to do and stay in your lane you will never work another day in your life. Simply put, you will be so fulfilled until you will not necessarily feel like you are working. Your sense of fulfillment will keep you desirous of completing your assigned purpose. You must stay in your lane and allow yourself to reach your fullest potential so that you will bring God glory. Additionally, when you stay in your lane you are less frustrated, you experience less stress, and you are less likely to be irritated. In fact, you will probably experience some of the most rewarding days of your life.

Remember the women executives in the previous chapter were gainfully employed, though they were unfulfilled. They were receiving definitive paychecks, but their jobs were not providing fulfillment. So, they resigned. Notice that these executives stayed in their lanes, but it became necessary to switch partners. Instead of working for someone, they utilized the same expertise to become entrepreneurs, and then they were fulfilled. They began networking with other entrepreneurs, which increased their exposure, elevated their platforms and afforded some worldwide travel opportunities. All because they were doing what they love in their lane. Their passion was very evident. These executives began to mentor others, teach their specialties, and provide workshops, seminars, and master classes frequently. And of course, this sharpened their skill sets, and expertise.

When you are in your lane, you have more flexibility and you are much more effective. You may find yourself working even harder or allowing your creativity to soar above mediocrity. Passion may keep you excited and motivated beyond your wildest imagination. Look at the analogy of a large trucking company. There are usually many trucks that deliver freight. Can you imagine the chaos everyone would experience if the terminal manager did not assign parking spaces for their drivers? That can be a very hectic scenario. Each trucker generally has an assigned space on the loading dock. Therefore, the truckers must park in their assigned space to load and offload freight. This method saves time, provides order and it should increase productivity. In essence, no one must run around the dock to locate a specific truck to load or offload. The dock workers simply have to report to the assigned space of the specific truck. Each trucker must stay in their lane (assigned parking space) to effectuate order, effective time management and increased productivity. When each trucker parks in their assigned lane the company is more likely to dispatch drivers to their appointments in a timelier manner. Timely deliveries usually mean satisfied customers. What a win-win situation!

These executives continue to soar in their lanes of expertise crushing their goals, and breaking glass ceilings. Though they may occasionally experience some very challenging times, they realize that they cannot afford to take their eyes off their goal; and they also realize that quitting is not an option. Therefore, they must push past the pain and stay in their lane to fulfill their purpose. They refuse to run or back up from growth pains. They realize that growth pains hurt, but they help. Mothers usually experience labor pains or contractions before they give birth. As time progresses, the contractions may become stronger and closer. Mothers PUSH as instructed to assist in the birthing process. Finally, the baby is born, and the pain is forgotten. The same scenario is true for these executives pressing into new arenas and new territory throughout the world. Yes, they encountered very demanding schedules, time management, travel arrangements, and more. However, they continued to persevere in their lane until they reached their goals.

Today these executives are awesome local, national, and global leaders positively impacting the world by staying in their lanes. They are much stronger and more resilient since fine-tuning their lanes to become awesome trailblazers. They show up to the table in some of the most unexpected places. Meghan (born Rachel Meghan Markle), Duchess of Sussex, who is biracial, recently made history when she wed Prince Harry. Until recently this was taboo. However, this was one of the most beautiful and unique wedding ceremonies in royal history. The recent elections produced some historical results. Prince George's County just elected its first African American, female, County Executive, Angela Alsobrooks. Sherri Allgood made history when she was elected as the first African American mayor in Montgomery County. Cynthia Marshall recently became the first African American female CEO in the NBA when she became the CEO of the Dallas Mavericks. That is only the beginning. Women are now speaking up, speaking out and speaking truth to power as never before.

So, continue to believe that you can do what you set out to do, set S.M.A.R.T. goals, discover what you love to do and stay in your lane. Stay in your lane no matter what others say. Once you know, that you know, that you know, that you know you are running in your assigned lane just keep it moving. This race is quite different from a marathon, because in a marathon the objective is to run with speed to win. However, your objective here is not speed, but staying within your specific parameters to meet your goal. Stay laser-focused on staying in your lane. It is imperative that as I said previously, you shut out the noisome pestilences, the naysayers, and anything or anyone that will break your focus. This is not about keeping up with the Joneses, but it is about extreme discipline that will allow you to be declared the winner. As a rule, the phrase staying in your assigned lane often applies to one's driving and trying to remain safe in the midst of some very interesting motorists or drivers. According to the Urban Dictionary, *"staying in your lane"* means mind your own business; keep moving forward in your own life and don't veer over into another person's personal affairs, don't be nosey or insert yourself in someone else's life, business or relationships.

Judge Karen Mills-Francis, the former Miami Dade County Court Judge and star of television's syndicated show Judge Karen's Court is known for the phrase, *"stay in your lane."* Remember that it is not enough to run a race, but it is very important to run in your assigned lane. Staying in your lane is one way to ensure that you finish the course and fulfill your destiny or your purpose. Don't ever stop believing in yourself. Remain confident in what God has preordained for you before the foundation of the world. Max Lucado says, *"Stay in your lane. Nothing good happens when you compare and compete. God doesn't judge you according to the talents of others. He judges you according to yours! His yardstick for measuring faithfulness is how faithful you are with your own gifts."* Be faithful and run your race as you stay in your lane.

Most of us have watched the Olympics where marathons are run frequently. Before the race begins each runner is cognizant of their boundaries, territory, or lane assignment. One of the most important rules is the fact that you must run within the confinement of your lane. Each runner is keenly aware of their assigned lane and does everything within their power to stay within the parameters of their assignment. That is exactly what you must do if you expect to meet your goal. I would like to suggest the following strategies to ensure that you stay in your lane.

In order to accomplish your mission to get motivated and achieve your goal you must always run with your goal in mind. Keep your goal on your radar. Never lose sight of it. Come rain, hail, sleet, snow, you must keep your goal in mind. Do not allow anyone to enter your arena and attempt to steer you in another direction; especially since your race was custom designed for you. Don't allow anyone but God to tell you what you can and cannot do. If you allow people to label you, then they may try to limit you. All the variables may look the same in your race and someone else's; however, the timing of events, the players that enter into your life, your faith in who and what God has called you to make a huge difference in your results and those ascribed to others. Therefore, run with your personal goal in mind. It does not matter if others feel that you are making a huge mistake. Keep running your race and stay in your lane. When you feel as if you may not be able to put one foot ahead of the other, keep running your race one step at a time and stay in your lane. When all hell seems to break loose and it seems to be a Murphy's Law Day, everything that can go wrong, goes wrong, run your race and stay in your lane. Eat your elephant one bite at a time. Step by step run your race, stay in your lane and accomplish your goal. There will be days when you run more, and there will be some when you run less. No worries, you are not in a competition with anyone else. However, you may find that you are in competition with yourself because discipline is not always easy. The Apostle Paul shares his challenge with us in Romans 7:17-25 KJV:

[17] Now then it is no more I that do it but sin that dwelleth in me.
[18] For I know that in me (that is, in my flesh,) dwelleth no good thing: for to will is present with me; but how to perform that which is good I find not.
[19] For the good that I would I do not: but the evil which I would not, that I do.
[20] Now if I do that I would not, it is no more I that do it, but sin that dwelleth in me.
[21] I find then a law, that, when I would do good, evil is present with me.
[22] For I delight in the law of God after the inward man:
[23] But I see another law in my members, warring against the law of my mind, and bringing me into captivity to the law of sin which is in my members.
[24] O wretched man that I am! who shall deliver me from the body of this death?
[25] I thank God through Jesus Christ our Lord. So then with the mind I myself serve the law of God; but with the flesh the law of sin.

So be encouraged because you are not the only one who faces challenges. Run your race, stay in your lane and get to the finish line. You are worth it. You deserve to shine; you deserve to be your best YOU. You deserve to reach your full potential. Therefore, press toward your goal daily. Believe God's promises and know that He loves you with an everlasting love according to Jeremiah 31:3. Know that you are fearfully and wonderfully made according to Psalm 139:14 KJV:

^{14} I will praise thee; for I am fearfully and wonderfully made: marvelous are thy works; and that my soul knoweth right well.

You are marvelous in His sight; so, focus on improving your weaknesses and reaching your God-given potential that will result in the most amazing sense of fulfillment that you can experience.

The next thing you need to do to accomplish your mission to get motivated and achieve your goal you must **always run focused on your future and not the past**. Once again, we can look at the Apostle Paul's writings in Philippians 3:13-14:

^{13}Brethren, I count not myself to have apprehended: but this one thing I do, forgetting those things which are behind, and reaching forth unto those things which are before,
^{14} I press toward the mark for the prize of the high calling of God in Christ Jesus.

It is imperative that you leave all negativity, disappointments, rejection, criticism, and frustration behind. You will be required to unpack all unnecessary baggage in order to grow and reach your goal. Allow God to stretch you into a new avenue or arena.

Especially since you are attempting to do something you have never done. That will require you to go where you have never gone, to become who you have never become. This will be unchartered territory as you embark upon a new venture, new ground and a new arena. Along with your newness you may feel slightly uncomfortable, or at times you may feel uncertain. However, this does not mean that you are not going in the right direction. **First and foremost, believe in the God in you**. He that promised is faithful. And when He could not find anyone else to swear by, He swore by Himself to ensure the integrity of His promise or guarantee. We can find this promise in Hebrews 6:13-14.

> *¹³For when God made promise to Abraham, because he could swear by no greater, he swore by himself,*
> *¹⁴ Saying, surely blessing I will bless thee, and multiplying I will multiply thee.*

So, press on toward your goal, because God's Word is out on you. Rest assured that He places His Word above His name as seen in Psalm 138:2:

> *²for thou hast magnified thy word above all thy name.*

Now that you have read one of God's promises to bless you and you have seen His guarantee, the next thing to do is believe GOD because He is not a man to lie. Because GOD said it, it must come to past, and it must manifest. Remember He swore by Himself. Then believe in the GOD in you. Never ever stop believing in yourself. Prepare for the journey and remember that it may not necessarily be the easiest thing to do. But it is not impossible.

Matthew 16:26 reminds us that *"WITH GOD ALL THINGS ARE POSSIBLE."*

²⁶Jesus looked at them and said, "With man this is impossible, but with God all things are possible.

And remember that ALL leaves out no thing, or nothing.

Another thing that you need to do in order to accomplish your mission to get motivated and achieve your goal is to steer clear of dream-killers. These are the individuals that may come as wolves dressed in sheep's clothing. They may pretend to cheer you on and celebrate you. However, they have no real interest in seeing you succeed or surpass them. These individuals will come along in many cases to sit in your front row to steal your thunder and pretend that they have your back, but they are really backstabbers in many instances. Or they may be tagging along to see if you fail. I know that is sad to say, but it is the truth. In some cases, these individuals may have attempted to do what you are presently doing but they failed. So, they may get an adrenaline rush while watching you attempt to surpass them.

We basically have three types of friends in life: Friends for a reason, friends for a season, and friends for a lifetime. Regardless of the reason people are following you, be sure you categorize them properly. Know your core support group of friends or your inner circle. This is the small ride for life group that will always be there for you. This is the group that you can depend on regardless of the time of day, night, location, or what you need; they will be there for you. This group will not allow anyone to talk about you without coming to your defense. This group is connected to your heart string. **You can always depend on them**. Everyone needs someone of this caliber in their circle. However, let me hasten to say that this place is reserved for those who have your best interest at heart at all times. This inner circle is not for those who want to flatter you, or tell you what you want to hear, so allow the Holy Spirit to lead you to those persons who deserve to be in your core support group especially because they will have the opportunity to witness your kaleidoscope of emotions, your highs and your lows. But they will still be there for you.

Bishop T.D. Jakes talks about three different groups of people in our lives: confidants, comrades, and constituents. The confidants are those people who are for you no matter what. If you have two or three confidents in a lifetime, consider yourself blessed. They love you unconditionally, cry with you and rejoice with you. They are there to ensure that you reach your destiny. They are your true ambassadors. Your constituents stand for what you stand for but are not for you. In other words, you have a common denominator that can be agreed upon. Your comrades stand for what you are against. You can use them to fight for you. You can win many sweatless victories when you use your comrades in the best possible manner. You must remember two important facts—constituents will leave you, and comrades will surely leave, but rest assured that confidants support you until the last bell has been rung, until the "fat lady has sung the last note," and you have been declared the winner by unanimous decision.

Therefore, ensure that you have reserved your front row for those who applaud you and who deserve a seat. Once you discover the dream-killers, please ensure that they are seated appropriately. This will alleviate getting sidetracked from your goal. Remember dream killers sometimes disguise themselves as wolves dressed in sheep's clothing. Therefore, do not be taken off focus by the family member who pretends to support you when their motive is to sabotage your mission. They may volunteer to help you do this, and that, but they really have an ulterior motive. They want you to fail. So, allow the Holy Spirit to reveal their heart. In St. John 16:13 the Holy Spirit is tasked with leading you, guiding you, and showing you things to come.

[13] Howbeit when He, the Spirit of truth, is come, He will guide you into all truth: for He shall not speak of Himself; but whatsoever He shall hear, that shall He speak: and He will shew you things to come.

Not only will you have family who may attempt to sabotage you, but there may also be some fake friends who set out to do the same. Steer clear of these dream-killers. Walk according to Proverbs 13:20 and be wise.

[20] He that walketh with wise men shall be wise: but a companion of fools shall be destroyed.

While you are attempting to stay in your lane you may need to tune out the noisome pestilences of frustration that constantly whisper in your ears, *"How long will it take before you reach your goal? You are tired, just quit. You can't do it."* BUT tune out any and everything that will not allow you to reach your goal. It is almost certain that you will get tired at some point in time. However, quitting is not an option. You can rest, but **DON'T QUIT!**

CHAPTER FOUR REFLECTIONS

➤ How does Urban Dictionary define "staying in your lane"?

_____
_____
_____
_____
_____
_____
_____
_____

➤ Name ways that will help you stay in your lane:

_____
_____
_____
_____
_____
_____
_____
_____
_____
_____

➤ Name and explain the dream killers you need to avoid:

_____
_____
_____
_____
_____
_____
_____
_____

➢ Explain the 3 categories of people Bishop Jakes talks about that come into our lives:

_____

PERSONAL NOTES

Chapter Five
Keep It Moving

Don't allow anyone to deter your focus.

Now that you are familiar with the parameters of your lane, and the dream killers that you need to avoid, you can keep moving and continue to run **your** race. At this point in time it is simply a matter of pacing yourself. All the preliminaries have been handled, the rules have been set, you are aware of your confidantes, your comrades and your constituents and your front row is reserved for your awesome cheerleaders. The most important thing for you to do is to run in your assigned lane, looking unto Jesus the author and finisher of your faith as stated in Hebrews 12:2:

² Looking unto Jesus the author and finisher of our faith; You can run because you have a Good Shepherd who loves you.

Psalm 23 (KJV)

¹ The Lord is my Shepherd; I shall not want.
² He maketh me to lie down in green pastures: He leadeth me beside the still waters.
³ He restoreth my soul: He leadeth me in the paths of righteousness for His name's sake.
⁴ Yea, though I walk through the valley of the shadow of death, I will fear no evil: for thou art with me; thy rod and thy staff they comfort me.

⁵ Thou preparest a table before me in the presence of mine enemies: thou anointest my head with oil; my cup runneth over.
⁶ Surely goodness and mercy shall follow me all the days of my life: and I will dwell in the house of the Lord forever.

This has always been one of my Psalms of encouragement. And I would not be surprised if it is yours as well. However, to help you keep it moving I would like to share a slightly modified version that you may personalize and add to your encouraging affirmations.

The Lord *is* my Shepherd, I shall not want. Notice that I didn't say the government or my husband of 45 years, but THE Lord Jesus is my personal shepherd right now **in this present time**. The word "is" denotes the present tense. Because He is my Shepherd, I have a relationship with Him. I can talk with Him throughout the day, when I come boldly to the throne of grace. There, I expect to find grace and mercy to help in my very time of need. What a relationship based upon His unconditional love for me. **I shall not want! That's abundance** because He has promised in Philippians 4:19 to supply my every need one by one as I walk upright in His Word, His Will, and His Way. The Good Shepherd desires that His sheep have only the best. God provides my every need. In fact, He is my source and total resource.

He maketh me to lie down in green pastures—**That's rest**. Have you ever been tired or exhausted? Once you took time to rest you felt so refreshed and revived. That's what our Shepherd does for us. He provides sweet rest especially when we cast our every care upon Him. He is the man for the job, and since He will be up all night anyway, cast your care upon Him, and allow Him to bless you to lie down in green pastures.

He leadeth me beside the still waters—**That's refreshment.** I can recall feeling so refreshed after drinking a cold glass of water on a very hot day. That is what our Shepherd does. He provides refreshment when the need arises.

He restoreth my soul—That's healing. All have sinned and come short of the glory of God. But we can confess our sins (I John 1:9), turn from them and have restored fellowship with God. That fellowship can fill us with incomparable joy and peace. Allow Him to give you new thoughts, and ideas. And of course, He heals us physically. Psalm 107:20 reminds us that He sent His Word and healed us.

He leadeth me in the paths of righteousness—That's guidance. Once we accept the Lord Jesus as our Master, Ruler and Controller, we have a blessed assurance in Psalm 32:8 which states *"I will instruct thee and teach thee in the way which thou shalt go: I will guide thee with mine eye."* Therefore, when we follow Him, we reach our destination safely. You cannot do it alone, but you can do ALL things through Christ who strengthens you daily. With the Lord on your side you will be empowered and motivated to reach your goal. Knowing that the Almighty God is for you is enough to keep you moving when you may feel like quitting. So, run looking forward. The goal is ahead, so look in that direction. It doesn't matter what is behind you, because you have legions of attentive angels to keep you in all your ways. Those angels are so attentive that they bear you up in their hands least you dash your foot against a stone. So, run, because goodness and mercy have your hind parts covered.

He just doesn't lead us in the path of righteousness, but He does it—<u>For His Namesake</u>—That's purpose. Jeremiah 29:11 says, *"For I know the thoughts that I think toward you, saith the Lord, thoughts of peace, and not of evil, to give you an expected end."* Since He created us, surely, He knows His expectations of us.

<u>Yea, though I walk through the valley of the shadow of death</u>— That's testing. We all have challenges in life. The Word of God says that many are the afflictions of the righteous, **but the Lord shall deliver Him out of them all**. So, make no mistake about, we're in a fixed fight but we have been declared the winner by unanimous decision—The Father, The Son, and the Holy Spirit. GLORY!

<u>I will fear no evil</u>—That's protection. Psalm 91:15 says, *"I will be with him in trouble; I will deliver him, and honour him."* Not only will our Great God deliver us, but He will HONOR us.
<u>I WILL NOT FEAR, FOR THOU ART WITH ME</u>—That's faithfulness. We can count on God, because He never reneges on a promise. His Word says, *"God is not a man to lie, if He said it, He is well able to bring it to pass."*

<u>Thy Rod and thy staff they comfort me</u>—That's discipline. These symbols can be applied to the life of a Christian when considering God's protection and correction in our lives. The verse states, *"your rod and your staff, they comfort me."* We should find comfort in the fact that our Shepherd (God) protects us from evil. Sometimes it may be more difficult to find comfort in the fact that God corrects us, but if you consider that the shepherd is much smarter than the sheep (God knows more than we will ever know) and knows what dangers lie around the corner, then we should be able to take comfort in the fact that our Shepherd guides us.

Thou preparest a table before me in the presence of mine enemies—That's hope. In the midst of great trouble, distress and affliction, in an orderly way, God prepares and organizes a long table of provision (nothing missing) and sustenance for each of us—for you and for me. When you are going through a time of trouble and distress, remind God what His Word says about taking care of you. Before one jot or tittle of His Word shall fail, heaven and earth shall pass away.

Thou anointest my head with oil—That's consecration! It is wonderful to be set apart for the Master's use and purpose.

My Cup runneth over—THAT'S ABUNDANCE! Not just enough but MORE THAN ENOUGH! **Surely (TRULY/DEFINITELY) goodness and mercy shall follow me all the days of my life—That's a cup overflowing with blessings!**

And I will dwell in the house of the Lord (MORTGAGE FREE) FOREVER—THAT'S SECURITY! GLORY TO GOD! PARDON ME WHILE I SHOUT!
With these wonderful provisions you can surely keep it moving looking forward to your goal. After you have successfully achieved your initial goal, repeat this process:

- **BELIEVE IN YOURSELF**
- **SET S.M.A.R.T. GOALS**
- **DO WHAT YOU LOVE**
- **STAY IN YOUR LANE; AND**

- **KEEP IT MOVING.**

These steps will help guide you clearly to the finish line. It does not matter what the goal is, just follow these same steps and you will be declared the winner by unanimous decision.

CHAPTER FIVE REFLECTIONS

➢ Name some preliminaries you handled to keep it moving:

_____
_____
_____
_____
_____
_____
_____
_____
_____
_____
_____
_____
_____
_____

➢ How has the 23rd Psalm impacted you?

_____
_____
_____
_____
_____
_____
_____
_____
_____
_____
_____
_____
_____

➢ How has the modified version of the 23rd Psalm impacted you?

PERSONAL NOTES

Conclusion

It has been my pleasure to encourage you by sharing some very important steps to help you get motivated to reach your goals. You are not the only one who has started a project, an assignment or a goal, but somehow became stuck. Once you adopt these principles, you can rest assured that you will not only set goals, but you will accomplish them. You will love the confidence that you have developed as a result of achieving and accomplishing simultaneous goals. You will walk with your head held high, your shoulders squared with a beautiful radiant smile on your face because of your newly accomplished goals.

This project began during a very challenging period in my life. I was sitting in my office when I felt the Holy Spirit leading me to begin writing. I had not planned to write a book at that time, BUT GOD had words of encouragement that I needed to share. Though this encourager needed someone to encourage her, God asked me to forget about my challenges and encourage others. So, I began to write as the Holy Spirit dictated. While writing I had a serious health challenge, but I stood on the Word of God for one year and healing manifested. I refused to quit despite facing several attacks of the enemy. I knew without a shadow of a doubt that GOD had given me the assignment of encouraging His precious children. The completion of this project has proven beyond a shadow of a doubt that GOD IS FAITHFUL! Therefore, I am blessed to give GOD ALL praise, glory, and honor for HIS faithfulness.

Lastly, allow me to be the first to congratulate you for taking a huge step toward accomplishing your goals by purchasing this book. Thank you very much and God bless you!

Appendix A

Motivation Quiz

How Motivated Are You?

This quick quiz gives you an idea of how motivated you are currently. Complete for your results, plus get great tips to get you more inspired and focused and see how your coach can assist.

INSTRUCTIONS: Think about your goals, then answer the questions by selecting the response CLOSEST to how you feel in your life *currently*. And remember that the answer you select is just an indicator—there are no right and wrong answers.

1. Can you visualize or imagine the benefits of this goal for YOU?

    a. Yes, I can clearly see, hear, imagine, feel the rewards I will get by achieving my goal.
    b. I know what the benefits might be, but I can't quite imagine achieving them.
    c. No, I find it hard to imagine things being different.

2. How prepared are you to make changes to your life to achieve your goals?

    a. I'm ready to do whatever I need to do to make it happen.
    b. I'd like to see how much I can achieve. I'm busy, but I am ready to make some effort.
    c. I'm not ready to make big changes yet. I have too much going on to change much.

3. How passionate are you about achieving your goals?

    a. Absolutely, I want it more than anything else right now!

b. I want to get there, but at my own pace.
c. A little—If I can make a small change, then I will be happy.

4. How much support would you like with the planning and execution of your goals?

a. I would love support in specific areas (e.g. Brainstorming, action planning, identifying obstacles, accountability).
b. Some support is good. If I plan, then I am more likely to stick to it.
c. I need some help to get started.

5. Do you persevere? How much willpower do you have?

a. When I set my mind to do something, I achieve it.
b. It varies. I have good days, but sometimes life gets in the way. I get distracted or tempted off-track.
c. Not much. I have often given up in the past due to a lack of willpower or commitment.

YOUR SCORES

	a's	b's	c's
TOTALS			

Your Motivation Quiz Results

MOSTLY A's - The Big Leap!
✓ You are well-motivated, organized, determined and keen to make changes.

PROS: You will achieve your goals one way or another, and if you don't there's always a very good reason.

CONS: You may be so focused on achieving your goals that you forget to celebrate, enjoy the journey or let other things in your life slip. Also, goals are sometimes easier to achieve when we slow down, letting things flow rather than pushing.

Ask your coach to help you: Look at your life balance. Are you relaxing and having enough fun? How could you enjoy achieving your goals more? Is there an easier way to achieve your goals? Your coach may also help you connect to yourself: What's most important to you in life? How do you want to feel once you've completed this goal? Is this goal what you really want, or is it for someone else? Where do you sabotage your "self"? Your coach may even ask you to stretch your goal and make it bigger—because when it's a MORE exciting goal we sometimes achieve it faster!

MOSTLY B's - The Middle Way!
✓ When a goal is big and important enough you take action, but like most people you occasionally struggle to stay focused and motivated. You have a full life and probably know what works for you, but are you set in your ways? Your motivation may vary as you're unsure how change would fit into your life. This means that sometimes you let life live you rather than actively creating the life you want.

PROS: Life is predictable and safe (even if busy). You mostly feel settled and may have good "life balance".

CONS: It's easy to get nice and settled in your comfort zone. But we also take longer to achieve our goals because we don't have the motivation, clarity, organization, energy and/or support we need to go the extra mile.

Ask your coach to help you: Get super clear on why you want your goals, so you're more inspired to take action! Make a plan! Get committed and take regular action. Also, ask your coach to help you identify where you self-sabotage and put steps in place for when you go off-track. If you're set in your comfort zone, ask your coach to stretch you and help you find new, exciting directions. If your "comfort" zone means you're constantly rushing around, ask your coach to help you with life balance, getting more organized and saying, "no." Your coach may also look at things like what zaps your time and energy and creating positive, healthy habits to make you even more effective.

MOSTLY C's - Small Steps...

- ✓ Perhaps you're happy with your life and your goals are simply a fine-tuning exercise.
- ✓ Or perhaps you're not really enjoying your life and are struggling to get moving on your goals. Maybe you can't see the benefits of your goals enough. Maybe your life is simply too busy and overwhelming or maybe you've been going after the wrong goals.

PROS: If you only want your life to be a little different, then small steps are the perfect way to hone and shape your life the way you want it. Change rarely happens overnight and taking it slow also lets you fit change into a super busy life. Setting and achieving smaller goals can also motivate us to go for something bigger next time! Finally, taking it slow helps us reconnect to ourselves and figure out what we really want.

CONS: Smaller steps obviously mean a goal takes longer to complete. Sometimes we lose momentum or motivation because progress is so slow! And it's unlikely you'll see big changes without putting more effort in.

Ask your coach to help you: Get to know yourself and what you want from life. What makes your heart sing? Even if your time and energy is limited, your coach can help you figure out goals that truly inspire you. A coach can help you break your goals down into measurable steps and create an action plan that works—holding you accountable and celebrating your progress. Your coach may also help you look at limiting beliefs, self-sabotaging habits, your lifestyle and life balance, values, and encourage you to think bigger so you can have a life you're really excited about.

Anyone—however busy—can make the life changes they need, with patience, understanding, determination and support! **A 10,000-mile journey starts with a single step**, and ALL action—however small—either moves you forwards or teaches you something. So, what are you waiting for?

Boost Your Motivation Homework:

- **Awe:** Sometimes life feels like it's just one action after another. When and what did you last wonder or marvel at?
- **Images can be powerful:** Think of a symbol, object or word that represents your goal and INSPIRES you (e.g. a role model, a glossy fruit bowl, a mountain, an animal). What qualities does your object have that you'd like more of? Now put a picture someplace where you will see it regularly (e.g. car, computer screen, mirror, wallet, fridge door etc.).
- **Get to know yourself:** Start a journal and record what motivates you (or doesn't) during your day and give them a score from 1 to 10: __ /10. Review and notice the activities, patterns and habits that boost, and get in the way of, your success!

Appendix B
S.M.A.R.T. Goal Setting Worksheet

Step 1: Write down your goal in as few words as possible.

My goal is to:
_____
_____
_____
_____

Step 2: Make your goal detailed and SPECIFIC.

Answer WHO/WHAT/WHERE/HOW/WHEN?
_____
_____
_____
_____
_____
_____
_____
_____
_____
_____
_____
_____
_____
_____
_____
_____
_____
_____
_____
_____

HOW will you reach this goal? List at least 3 action steps you'll take (be specific):

1.
_____
_____
_____
_____

2.
_____
_____
_____
_____

3.
_____
_____
_____
_____

Step 3: Make sure your goal is MEASUREABLE.

Add details, measurements and tracking details. I will measure/track my goal by using the following numbers or methods:

_____
_____
_____
_____
_____
_____
_____

I will know I've reached my goal when:

Step 4: Make your goal ATTAINABLE.

What additional resources do you need for success? Items I need to achieve this goal:

How I'll find the time:

Things I need to learn more about:

People I can talk to for support:

Step 5: Make your goal REALISTIC.

List *why* you want to reach this goal:

Step 6: Make your goal TIMELY.

Put a deadline on your goal and set some benchmarks.

Appendix C
Encouraging Scriptures

Philippians 4:6-7 "Be careful for nothing; but in everything by prayer and supplication with thanksgiving let your requests be made known unto God. And the peace of God, which passeth all understanding, shall keep your hearts and minds through Christ Jesus."

Jeremiah 29:11 "For I know the thoughts that I think toward you, saith the Lord, thoughts of peace, and not of evil, to give you an expected end."

Proverbs 3:5-6 "Trust in the Lord with all thine heart; and lean not unto thine own understanding. In all thy ways acknowledge him, and he shall direct thy paths."

Psalm 46:10 "Be still and know that I am God."

Galatians 6:9 "And let us not be weary in well doing: for in due season we shall reap, if we faint not."

Matthew 6:33 "But seek ye first the kingdom of God, and his righteousness; and all these things shall be added unto you."

Matthew 7:7 "Ask, and it shall be given you; seek, and ye shall find; knock, and it shall be opened unto you."

Romans 8:28 "And we know that all things work together for good to them that love God, to them who are the called according to his purpose."

Jeremiah 33:3 "Call unto me, and I will answer thee, and show thee great and mighty things, which thou knowest not."
Jeremiah 32:27 "Behold, I am the Lord, the God of all flesh: is there anything too hard for me?"

John 10:10 "I am come that they might have life, and that they might have it more abundantly."

Philippians 4:19 "But my God shall supply all your need according to his riches in glory by Christ Jesus."

Psalm 34:4 "I sought the Lord, and he heard me, and delivered me from all my fears."

Colossians 3:17 "And whatsoever ye do, do it heartily, as to the Lord, and not unto men."

About the Author

Dr. Mary J. Huntley

Everyone needs a coach to help them achieve their dreams and goals. I am honored to serve you in a Spirit of Excellence which includes integrity and honesty as a Board-Certified Master Life Coach. Allow me to help you devise a strategic action plan that will help you get laser-focused on your goals. I will utilize my expertise to help you avoid distractions, dream killers, and obstacles that will attempt to derail your purpose, destiny and vision.

During our time together, your confidence will receive a huge boost as you learn to speak truth to power and take your seat at the table with other leaders. You will refuse to remain silent when you know that you should show up, speak up and speak out.

LET'S CONNECT

www.drmaryjhuntley.com
Facebook: DrMary J Huntley
Twitter: drmaryj_huntley
Instagram: authordrmaryjhuntley
www.amazon.com/author/drmaryjhuntley

About the Publisher

Vision to Fruition Publishing House

At **Vision to Fruition Publishing House**, we are dedicated to helping others bring their personal, business, ministry and nonprofit visions to fruition.

Whether it's as grand as a book you want to write, a business you want to start, a conference or event you want to host, a ministry you want to launch or an organization you want to start; or as small as needing a computer repair, logo design or web design; **Vision to Fruition Publishing House** will help you walk through the process and set you up for success! At **Vision to Fruition** we don't have clients, we have **Visionaries**. We provide solutions to equip others to pursue their visions and dreams with reckless abandon.

We have published more than twenty-three authors, several of which were #1 Amazon Bestsellers. We would love for you to join our family of Visionaries as well!!!

Learn more here: www.vision-fruition.com

www.ingramcontent.com/pod-product-compliance
Lightning Source LLC
Chambersburg PA
CBHW071407290426
44108CB00014B/1714